Table of Contents

Tables

Figures

Preface

U.S. oil production has grown rapidly in recent years. U.S. Energy Information Administration (EIA) data, which reflect combined production of crude oil and lease condensate, show a rise from 5.6 million barrels per day (bbl/d) in 2011 to 7.4 million bbl/d in 2013. EIA's *Short-Term Energy Outlook* (STEO) projects continuing rapid production growth in 2014 and 2015, with forecast production in 2015 averaging 9.5 million bbl/d. While EIA's *Annual Energy Outlook* (AEO) projects further production growth, its pace and duration remain uncertain, as shown by the significant differences between Reference case and High Oil and Gas Resource case projections, which differ in both the timing and level of the highest volume of U.S. crude oil production. EIA's next update to the AEO will raise projected production significantly in the Reference case.

Recent and forecast increases in domestic crude production have sparked discussion on the topic of how rising crude oil volumes will be absorbed. Given the likelihood of continued growth in domestic crude production, and the recognition that some absorption options, such as like-for-like replacement of import streams, are inherently limited, the question of how a relaxation in current limitations on crude exports might affect domestic and international markets for both crude and products continues to hold great interest for policymakers, industry, and the public. In response to multiple requests, EIA is developing analyses that shed light on this question.

A change in current limitations on crude oil exports could have implications for both domestic and international crude oil prices. To the extent that current limitations on exports cause domestic crudes to sell at lower prices than could occur if those limitations were relaxed, such a relaxation could raise the price of domestically produced oil. If higher prices for domestic crude were to spur additional U.S. production than might otherwise occur, the increase to global crude oil supply could reduce the global price of crude. The extent to which domestic crude prices might rise, and global crude prices might fall, depends on a host of factors, including the degree to which current export limitations affect prices received by domestic producers, the sensitivity of future domestic production to price changes, the ability of domestic refiners to absorb domestic production, and the reaction of key foreign producers to changes in the level of U.S. crude production.

While crude oil prices matter to those involved in producing oil or refining oil into products, most Americans, and the policymakers who represent and serve them, are mainly concerned with the price of gasoline and other refined products. With U.S. gasoline consumption running at 8.8 million bbl/d and the average retail price of gasoline for all grades at $3.58 per gallon, the average American household spent $2,600 on gasoline in 2013. Recognizing that the possible relaxation of current export limitations could cause the prices of domestic and international crude grades to move in opposite directions (the former tending to rise, the latter tending to fall) one question of interest to policymakers and the public is which crude prices, domestic or international, matter most to the determination of gasoline prices in the United States. This paper focuses on that question, and also explores how linkages across regional and international markets where gasoline is sold have evolved over time and influence gasoline pricing in domestic markets.

U.S. Energy Information Administration | What Drives U.S. Gasoline Prices?

1

While the linkages that motivate the hypothesis that a relaxation of limitations on crude oil exports could cause domestic and international crude grades to move in opposite directions are briefly discussed above, the extent of any actual change in domestic production or the domestic or international price of crude oil that might follow from a relaxation of crude oil export limitations is not addressed in this paper. EIA is undertaking further analyses that will examine those issues and expects to report additional results over the coming months.

U.S. Energy Information Administration | What Drives U.S. Gasoline Prices?

2

Executive Summary

This analysis provides context for considering the impact of rising domestic light crude oil production on the price that U.S. consumers pay for gasoline, and provides a framework to consider how changes to existing U.S. crude oil export restrictions might affect gasoline prices.

Given the likelihood of continued growth in domestic crude production, and the recognition that some absorption options, such as like-for-like replacement of imported crude oil streams, are inherently limited, the possibility that a relaxation of current policy limitations on crude exports might affect domestic and international markets for both crude oil and products, particularly gasoline, is an important issue.

EIA's analysis of the factors affecting U.S. gasoline prices is twofold. The analysis first considers the relationship between U.S. spot gasoline prices and international and domestic spot crude oil prices, represented by Brent and West Texas Intermediate (WTI), respectively. The second part of the analysis focuses on the interrelationship of U.S. and worldwide gasoline prices and the extent to which global gasoline prices are important in determining U.S. gasoline prices. This analysis takes into account regional and global gasoline supply/demand balances and arbitrage, as well as how the competitive advantage of U.S. Gulf Coast (USGC) refineries is changing the dynamics of U.S. regional and global gasoline pricing.

Key observations from EIA's analysis of the relationship between gasoline and crude oil prices include:

- Brent crude oil prices are more important than WTI crude oil prices as a determinant of U.S. gasoline prices in all four regions studied, including the Midwest.

- The effect that a relaxation of current limitations on U.S. crude oil exports would have on U.S. gasoline prices would likely depend on its effect on international crude oil prices, such as Brent, rather than its effect on domestic crude prices.

- The WTI crude oil price lost much of its power to explain changes in U.S. gasoline prices after 2010, when its differential to Brent crude became wider and more volatile.

- The Brent crude oil price lost very little of its power to explain changes in U.S. gasoline prices in the post-2010 period.

Key observations from EIA's analysis of global gasoline price relationships include:

- Gasoline is a globally traded commodity and, as a result, prices and changes in prices are highly correlated across global spot markets.

- Gasoline balances and flows around the world are changing.

    - Increasing demand in Asia, Latin America, and the Middle East has been outpacing increases in gasoline production in those regions.
    - Demand is declining in the United States, but refinery production of gasoline is rising, resulting in increases in U.S. exports of gasoline into the global market.

- Demand is declining in Europe, adding to its gasoline oversupply; excess European gasoline now competes with increased exports from the United States.
- Because of these changing supply and demand patterns, global gasoline price relationships are changing; USGC and Chicago spot gasoline prices, which are closely linked, are now often the lowest in the world during the fall and winter months.

- U.S. gasoline exports grew rapidly from 2009-2012 but have since leveled off; however, Gulf Coast gasoline is now being exported to more distant markets, routinely including Africa and, during the winter months, Asia.

Gasoline and Crude Oil Price Relationships

Part 1: The relationship between gasoline prices and crude oil prices

Crude oil is the main input cost in the production of gasoline, and changes in crude oil price, along with changes in gasoline market conditions, drive changes in wholesale and retail gasoline prices. EIA estimates that about two-thirds of the price of gasoline at the pump is attributable to the refinery cost of crude oil. When the price of crude oil changes, the price of wholesale gasoline adjusts concurrently to reflect the increased refinery input cost, other market factors being equal.

Past EIA research and analysis[1] has shown that changes in wholesale gasoline spot prices have a consistent and predictable effect on changes in retail gasoline prices. Other factors equal, a $1-per-barrel change in the price of crude oil will result in a $1-per-barrel, or $0.024-per-gallon (1/42 of $1 because there are 42 gallons in one barrel) change in the price of wholesale and retail gasoline. Statistical analysis demonstrates about half of the change in crude oil price is passed through to retail prices within two weeks of the price change, all other market factors equal.[2]

U.S retail gasoline prices are generally determined by four broad elements: 1) the price of crude oil, 2) refining costs and profit margins, 3) retail and distribution costs and profit margins, and 4) taxes.[3] Elements three and four compose the retail segment of the supply chain, and they tend to be relatively stable. Because this paper addresses how gasoline prices change over time, it focuses on the first two elements, which account for most of the variability in retail prices.

Prices for a wide array of crude oils and wholesale gasoline specifications are available in markets, or trading hubs, around the world. These prices are commonly called spot prices. The spot market is often the first pricing point for petroleum products such as gasoline. At this level, sales of product for immediate delivery take place at a convenient transfer point, such as a refinery, port, or pipeline junction. The spot price for a product reflects the cost of crude oil and other inputs to refiners as well as the costs and profits of processing that crude oil into products.[4]

Because the purchases and sales reflected by spot prices generally occur in actively traded markets with many participants, they very quickly reflect market supply and demand conditions for that commodity. It is this variability in crude oil prices and spot gasoline prices that causes most of the variation in retail gasoline prices.

Prior to 2011, the question of whether Brent was more or less significant than WTI in determining U.S. gasoline prices was not very important. Historically, the price spread between Brent and WTI was relatively narrow and consistent, reflecting the cost of moving light sweet crude from the North Sea or West Africa to the United States (Figure 1). However, beginning in mid-2010, growing deliveries of

---

[1] Gasoline Price Pass-through (January 2003): http://www.eia.gov/petroleum/archive/gasolinepass.htm

[2] While EIA recognizes that wholesale gasoline and crude oil prices are interdependent, because demand for crude oil is very highly related to the demand for refined products, this analysis focuses on the first order relationship between changes in crude oil price and wholesale gasoline price.

[3] http://www.eia.gov/petroleum/gasdiesel/pump_methodology.cfm

[4] *This Week In Petroleum* (November 24, 2010): http://www.eia.gov/petroleum/weekly/archive/2010/101124/twipprint.html

Canadian crude oil to Cushing, Oklahoma, and increasing U.S. light sweet crude oil production from tight oil formations, such as Bakken, Permian, and Eagle Ford, caused transportation bottlenecks in the U.S. Midcontinent. These bottlenecks caused the prices of U.S. crudes, like WTI, to decline compared with the prices of globally-traded crudes such as Brent. From 2011 through June 2014, weekly average WTI discounts to Brent ranged from $2 to $28 per barrel.

Graph removed due to copyright restrictions

Source: Bloomberg LP.

As WTI prices declined relative to Brent, U.S. gasoline prices generally maintained their previous relationship with Brent. From 2000 through 2010, the average annual spread between the U.S. average regular gasoline retail price and Brent spot price was $0.91 per gallon (Figure 2). From 2011 through 2013, the retail spread to Brent averaged $0.92 per gallon, almost unchanged from the 2000-2010 period. The relationship between spot gasoline in major markets across the United States and Brent also remained generally constant over the entire period.

Unlike the spread between gasoline and Brent, the spread between gasoline and WTI changed significantly when Brent and WTI prices diverged in 2011. From 2000 through 2010, the average annual spread between the U.S. average regular gasoline retail price and the WTI spot price was $0.87 per gallon.[5] However, from 2011 through 2013, the spread between the price of retail gasoline and WTI crude oil was significantly higher, ranging from $1.17 to $1.38 per gallon. In the United States, WTI

---

[5] During this period the highest average annual spread of $1.07 per gallon occurred in 2007 when global gasoline supply was extremely tight. The spread between gasoline and Brent was also $1.07 in 2007.

prices are more widely quoted than Brent prices by press and media outlets, and the price of WTI is often reported as *the* price of crude oil. As a result, the change from historical levels in the price difference between retail gasoline prices and WTI prompted questions about whether the relationship between crude oil and retail gasoline prices had changed. While not as visible to consumers, a similar shift occurred between the price of WTI and the spot price of gasoline at major markets across the United States.

The consistency over time of the pricing relationship between gasoline and Brent crude oil, and the apparent change in the pricing relationships between gasoline and WTI when Brent and WTI diverged significantly starting in 2011, suggest that Brent, rather than WTI, has been more important in determining U.S. gasoline prices.

Figure 2. Annual average retail gasoline to crude oil price spread

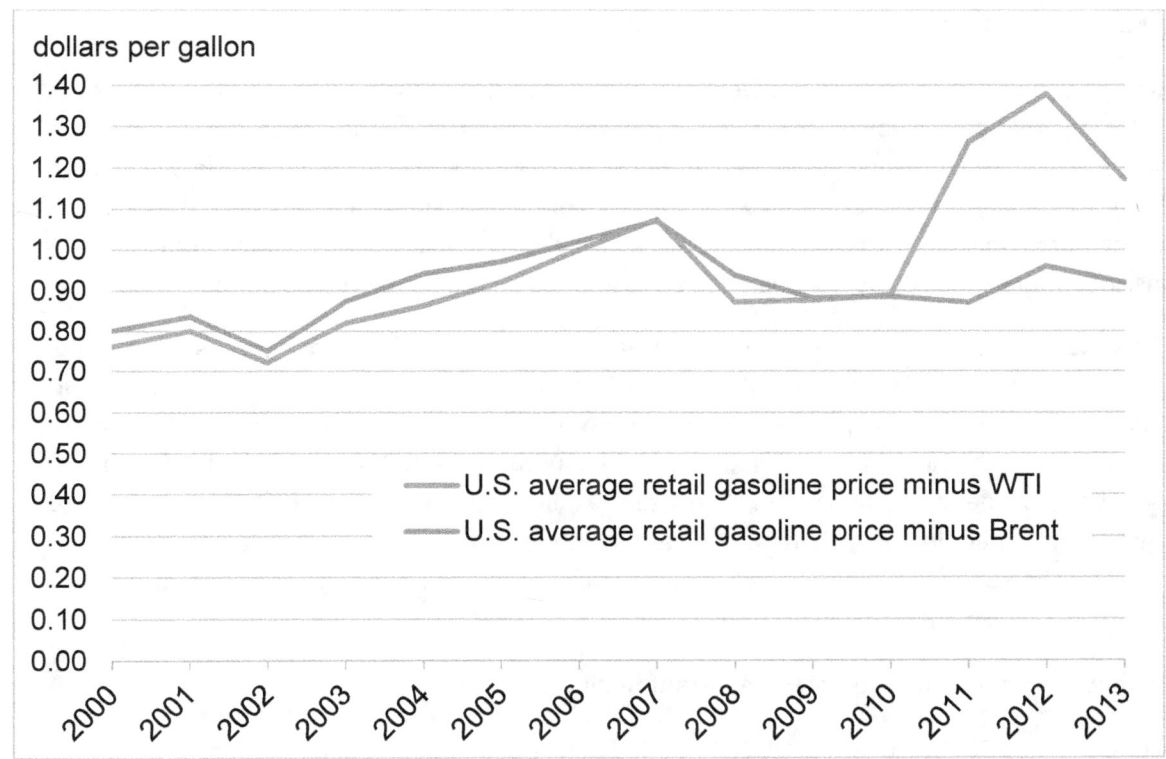

Source: U.S. Energy Information Administration and Thomson Reuters.

The issue of which crude oil matters most for U.S. gasoline prices is particularly relevant as policymakers in the Executive Branch and Congress consider the possibility of changes in current limitations on crude oil exports. To the extent that current limitations on exports cause domestic crudes to sell at lower prices than could occur if those limitations were relaxed, such a relaxation could raise the price of domestically produced oil. If higher prices for domestic crude were to spur additional U.S. production than might otherwise occur, the increase to global crude oil supply could reduce the global price of crude. The extent to which domestic crude prices might rise, and global crude prices might fall, depends on a host of factors, including the degree to which current export limitations affect prices received by domestic producers, the sensitivity of future domestic production to price changes, the ability of

U.S. Energy Information Administration | What Drives U.S. Gasoline Prices?

7

domestic refiners to absorb domestic production, and the reaction of key foreign producers to changes in the level of U.S. crude production.

The extent of any actual change in domestic production or the domestic or international price of crude oil that might follow from a relaxation of crude oil export limitations, which will be the subject of further analyses, is beyond the scope of this paper. However, the possibility that prices of domestic crudes, such as WTI, and international crudes, such as Brent, would move in opposite directions highlights the importance of understanding which type of crude drives U.S. gasoline prices, which may be the most salient petroleum product price for the public and many policymakers.

For this reason, EIA decided to undertake statistical modeling to dig deeper into the question of how gasoline prices are linked to various types of crude oil. Despite the evidence reviewed above suggesting that Brent was more important than WTI, EIA developed its statistical analysis in a symmetric fashion, running specifications for both Brent and WTI in parallel.

The analysis considers the relationship of weekly changes in spot gasoline prices in the four regions of the United States that have viable spot markets for gasoline (New York Harbor (NYH), USGC, Chicago, and Los Angeles) as a function of weekly changes in the spot price of Brent and WTI crude oils and the change in the deviation of regional gasoline inventories from the most recent five-year average level. The deviation in regional inventory was included as a proxy for regional gasoline supply-demand conditions. The period covered by the analysis begins in 2000 and continues through June 2014.

The analysis examines the gasoline-crude oil price relationships over two periods. The first period runs from 2000 through year-end 2010, a period when the Brent-WTI spread was consistently narrow. During the second period, which begins in January 2011 and continues through the end of June 2014, the Brent-WTI spread was typically wider and quite volatile. The econometric equations test how well Brent and WTI crude oil prices independently explain changes in gasoline prices in each of the two periods. They also examine whether adding the other crude oil as an independent variable (e.g., adding a Brent component into the equation where WTI is the explanatory variable) in the form of the Brent-WTI spread improves the explanatory power of the equation.

The econometric analysis supports three important findings:

1. For both the 2000-2010 and 2011-2014 periods, the equations in which the Brent price was used as the independent variable have more explanatory power than the equations in which WTI was the independent variable. This holds true for all regional markets, including the Midwest.
2. The equations that use Brent as the independent variable lose very little explanatory power from period one (2000-2010) to period two (2011-June 2014), while equations with WTI as the independent variable lose considerable explanatory power from period one to period two.
3. Introducing the Brent-WTI spread to equations in which WTI is the independent variable significantly improves the explanatory power of the equations, while introducing this spread to equations that use Brent as the independent variable does not significantly improve the explanatory power.

Together, these findings support the conclusion that the Brent crude oil price is more important than WTI crude oil price as a determinant of U.S. gasoline prices. The second conclusion shows that this was the case during both times of narrow and stable Brent-WTI spreads and times of relatively wide and volatile spreads.

A detailed discussion of the econometric analysis and results is included in the Statistical Methodology for Relationships between Gasoline and Crude Price appendix of this report.

Part 2: Global gasoline price relationships

The previous section shows that Brent prices, rather than WTI prices, are the main crude oil price determinant of spot, and therefore retail, U.S. gasoline prices. However, crude oil prices are not the sole determining factor for spot gasoline prices. Spot gasoline prices are also a function of the wholesale gasoline margin, often referred to as the gasoline crack spread, i.e., the difference between spot gasoline price and crude oil price. Wholesale gasoline margins take into account supply/demand conditions for gasoline at the prevailing crude oil price, including refining costs and refining profits. Together, the price of Brent crude oil and the wholesale gasoline margin in a given market compose that market's spot gasoline price.

The major markets for gasoline in the United States include NYH, the USGC, Chicago, and Los Angeles. Outside the United States, the major gasoline market hubs are Amsterdam-Rotterdam-Antwerp (ARA), the Mediterranean, and Singapore. NYH, the USGC, ARA, and the Mediterranean are part of the actively traded Atlantic Basin petroleum market. Chicago is directly linked to the Atlantic Basin market through infrastructure connections to the USGC. Singapore is a major trading hub in the Pacific Basin market, which also includes Los Angeles.

Prices at these different trading hubs are linked through arbitrage, and the differences between prices at different trading hubs reflect transportation costs between the regions, differences in gasoline quality, such as octane rating, and regional supply/demand balances. Gasoline moves from markets with surplus supply to markets in need of supply based on these price differences. This means that spot gasoline prices in markets that produce more gasoline than they consume, assuming no difference in quality specifications, need to be lower than prices in markets that consume more gasoline than they produce, in order to encourage gasoline to flow from the market with excess supply to the market in need of supply. In this way, the price of gasoline in different locations both in the United States and around the world is set by supply and demand conditions in the various regional markets that make up the global market.

Because the United States is an active participant in the global petroleum market as both an exporter and importer of gasoline, U.S. gasoline prices are tied to global gasoline prices. As quality specification differences among the major gasoline markets are relatively small, and because gasoline can be shipped between markets for a relatively low cost, the price differences among the major gasoline trading hubs tend to be small and price movements highly correlated (Figure 3).

Graph removed due to copyright restrictions

Source: Bloomberg LP and Thomson Reuters.

Changing global gasoline price relationships

Spot gasoline prices in NYH, ARA, and Singapore can be broadly thought of as being representative of the western Atlantic basin, the eastern Atlantic Basin, and the Pacific Basin, respectively. Prior to 2008, the United States, in particular the U.S. East Coast, was a large and growing gasoline market that needed to import large amounts of gasoline from the international market to meet demand. To attract gasoline supply to the U.S. East Coast from Europe, and at times from the Pacific Basin, NYH gasoline prices typically traded at a premium to prices in ARA and Singapore.

Around 2008, economic recession, efficiency policies, and U.S. ethanol mandates began eroding gasoline demand in the Atlantic Basin, while gasoline demand in Asia continued growing, led by major consuming countries China, India, and Indonesia. This shift in demand growth contributed to an increase in Singapore gasoline prices relative to prices in NYH and ARA. Since 2008, the price of gasoline in Singapore has typically been the highest price among the three major trading hubs, reflecting the need for gasoline supply to flow into the Pacific Basin (Figure 4). Despite the erosion in Atlantic Basin gasoline demand and the increase in demand in Asia, the relationship between gasoline prices in the ARA and NYH has remained relatively unchanged from the period before 2008. The stability of the ARA-NYH price relationship reflects the continuing need for the East Coast to import gasoline, much of which has been and continues to be supplied from northwest Europe.

Figure 4. New York Harbor gasoline spot price differentials to ARA and Singapore

Graph removed due to copyright restrictions

Source: Bloomberg LP and Thomson Reuters.

Both NYH and the USGC are submarkets in the western Atlantic Basin. The USGC, which is home to half of U.S. refining capacity and about 10% of total global refining capacity, has long been a major supplier of gasoline and other refined products to other regions of the United States. More recently, the USGC has become a major supplier to the rest of the world. The combination of increasing USGC production of refined products and stagnating Atlantic Basin demand has had a major impact on global gasoline markets.

Historically, USGC spot gasoline priced in a tight range with other Atlantic Basin and U.S. gasoline prices. From 2000 through 2010, USGC spot gasoline prices averaged a $0.07-per-gallon premium to ARA, reflecting the United States' status as a major gasoline importer. During the 2000-2010 period, USGC gasoline prices were slightly lower on average than NYH and Chicago, reflecting the region's position as a supplier to those markets. As was the case in other Atlantic Basin markets, in 2008, USGC prices shifted from typically being at a premium to Singapore to typically being at a discount, reflecting the easing supply-demand balances in the Atlantic Basin and the tightening balances in the Pacific Basin. Beginning in 2011, USGC gasoline prices began to price at a discount to prices at all other major market hubs for much of the calendar year, and the volatility of the spread between USGC gasoline prices and other global gasoline prices increased. USGC gasoline prices fell to a discount to ARA, NYH, and Singapore prices of $0.01, $0.10, and $0.13 per gallon, respectively, on average from January 2011 through June 2014. Additionally, USGC gasoline price discounts to other locations reached particularly wide levels during the past three winters when seasonally lower demand and record refinery runs in the

U.S. Energy Information Administration | What Drives U.S. Gasoline Prices?

11

United States substantially increased supply in the USGC gasoline market (Figure 5). As a result, the USGC exported an average of 436,000 bbl/d of total gasoline in 2013, up from 119,000 bbl/d in 2008. Monthly USGC gasoline exports reached a high of 659,000 bbl/d in December 2012.

Figure 5. U.S. Gulf Coast gasoline spot price differentials to NYH, ARA, and Singapore

Graph removed due to copyright restrictions

Source: Bloomberg LP and Thomson Reuters.

Changing U.S.gasoline supply patterns

Changes in regional supply-demand balances in both the USGC and the Midwest have contributed to changes in gasoline price relationships and supply flows. From 2008 through 2013, USGC petroleum-based (non-ethanol) gasoline consumption increased only modestly, and in the Midwest, consumption decreased by 100,000 bbl/d, largely due to increased ethanol blending and fleet efficiency gains as a result of corporate average fuel economy (CAFE) standards. Over the same period, access to price-advantaged crude oil and natural gas feedstock increased the relative competitiveness of U.S. refineries in the global market, as did refinery investment in upgrading capacity and capacity expansions. Since 2008, when USGC refinery production of gasoline bottomed out at 4.0 million bbl/d, refineries increased gasoline production to an average of almost 4.4 million bbl/d during 2013. Over the same period, Midwest refineries increased gasoline production from 1.8 million bbl/d to almost 2.0 million bbl/d. On an average annual basis, the USGC's surplus of gasoline production over consumption increased from 2.7 million bbl/d in 2008 to 3.0 million bbl/d in 2013. In the Midwest, the supply shortfall decreased by half, dropping from 0.6 million bbl/d in 2008 to just 0.3 million bbl/d in 2013 (Figure 6). Because the Midwest's shortfall of gasoline is supplied from the USGC, the reduction in the amount of gasoline needed to meet demand in the Midwest pushed gasoline supply back to the USGC, directly adding to supplies available on the USGC.

Figure 6. Monthly refinery production of gasoline minus regional consumption

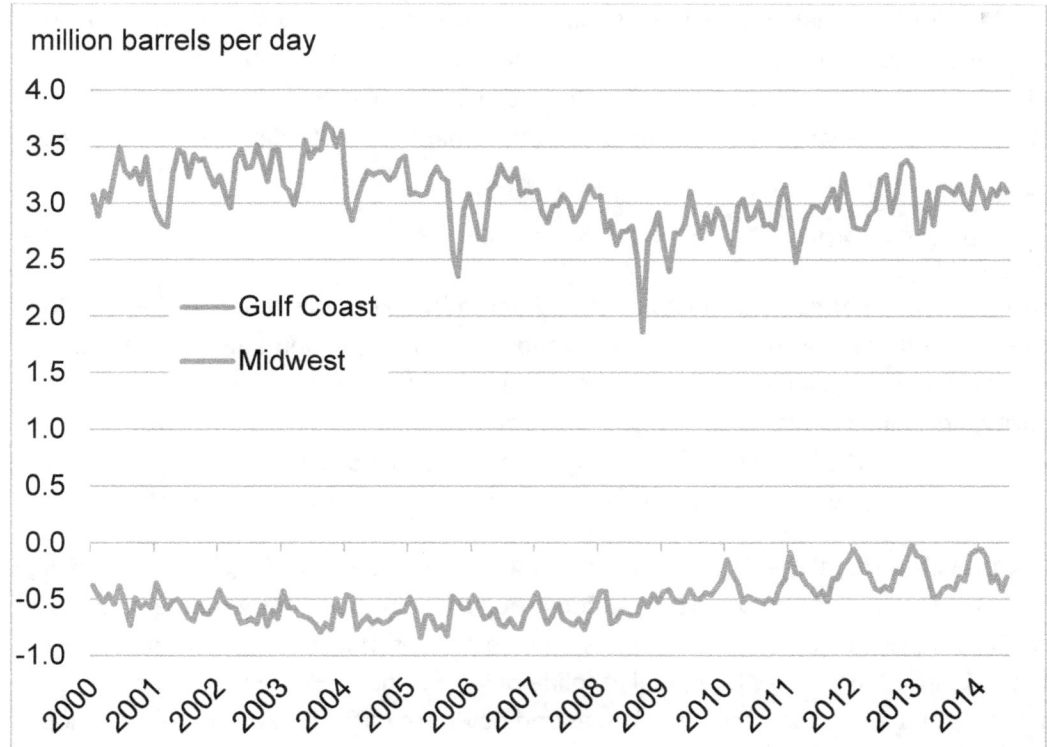

Source: U.S. Energy Information Administration, *Petroleum Supply Monthly*.

Because most incremental supply in the Midwest comes from the USGC, the reduction in USGC-produced gasoline needed to supply the Midwest, along with the increasing production on the USGC itself, combined to increase the annual average USGC supply relative to consumption by almost 0.6 million bbl/d since 2008.

USGC gasoline oversupply is particularly high during the winter months when gasoline demand in the United States is at a seasonal low. Again, the Midwest is a key driver of this dynamic. While Midwest gasoline production was 390,000 bbl/d below consumption on average from March–October 2013, the shortfall was just 90,000 bbl/d on average during the winter months of November 2013–February 2014. However, the dramatic narrowing of the gasoline production gap in the Midwest during the winter is a recent development. As recently as the winter months of November 2010–January 2011, the Midwest production shortfall averaged 270,000 bbl/d.

A combination of declines in demand and increases in refinery crude runs in the late autumn and early winter have increased gasoline oversupply in the USGC. From November 2013 to January 2014, USGC refinery gross inputs to distillation units were 8.3 million bbl/d, up almost 0.5 million from the same period in 2010-11. Much of this increase was the result of increased capacity rather than higher utilization of existing capacity. Utilization for USGC refineries remained unchanged at 91% over those periods. In the Midwest, gross inputs increased 0.2 million bbl/d from November 2010–January 2011 to average 3.5 million bbl/d from November 2013 to January 2014.

Although a lower call on USGC gasoline by the Midwest and more surplus gasoline production in the USGC have made more gasoline available on the USGC, pipeline infrastructure and marine shipping constraints limit how much USGC-produced gasoline can be economically transferred to other U.S. regions, particularly the U.S. East Coast, which produces less gasoline than it consumes. As a result, USGC refinery utilization is now very much a function of export demand, and USGC spot gasoline prices reflect the shift.

Changing global gasoline trade flows

As noted above, the differences between product prices at different market hubs reflect transportation costs between the regions, differences in gasoline quality, and regional supply-demand balances. As the USGC produces increasingly more gasoline than it consumes, the spot gasoline prices in the USGC have shifted to export parity, declining versus gasoline prices in Europe, Singapore, NYH, and the rest of the world, and encouraging the export of gasoline to the marginal market for USGC production. Spot gasoline prices in the USGC are now typically the lowest in the world for at least some part of the year.

Tables 1 and 2 below provide percentage data by month on the number of weeks the gasoline price in a particular market hub was the lowest among the identified group of major hubs. As gasoline typically flows from regions of lower price where there is excess supply to regions of higher price where supply is needed, these data can be used as a proxy for global gasoline balances and trade flows. Data on individual and aggregated global refined product balances and flows are difficult to accurately develop because of differences in the availability of country-level and regional data and concerns about data integrity. Table 1 covers the period 2000-2010 and the Table 2 the period 2011-14. These two time periods were chosen for consistency with the analysis of the relationship between U.S. gasoline prices and crude oil prices. The gasoline-crude analysis takes into account the observed January 2011 break point between the relationship of gasoline and crude oil prices that resulted from the decline in U.S. crude prices relative to global crude prices. The decline in U.S. crude oil prices, combined with access to low-cost natural gas, created incentives for U.S. refineries to increase crude runs leading to higher gasoline production. The combination of higher gasoline production and stagnating Atlantic basin gasoline demand resulted in changes in global gasoline price relationships.

Table 1. Percentage of weeks with lowest average weekly gasoline spot price 2000-10

Graph removed due to copyright restrictions

Source: Bloomberg LP and Thomson Reuters.

Table 2. Percentage of weeks with lowest average weekly gasoline spot price 2011-14

Graph removed due to copyright restrictions

Source: Bloomberg LP and Thomson Reuters.

As the data in Table 1 indicate, during the period 2000-2010, the lowest gasoline spot prices were most often in Europe and Singapore. The Singapore price was lowest particularly during the summer, although mostly prior to 2008. The price was less-frequently lowest at a U.S. market hub, and only in the USGC or Chicago. NYH and Los Angeles never had the lowest price.

In 2011, as the USGC gasoline supply surplus began to increase, the relationship between global gasoline prices began to change. As the data in Table 2 show, during the winter months of the 2011-through-

June-2014 period, the price of gasoline in the USGC or Chicago was most often the lowest, while the gasoline price in Europe was typically lowest during the spring and in July. Over the 2011–June 2014 period, the price of gasoline in Singapore was lowest less frequently and only during the June through October period. NYH was never the lowest price gasoline market because the region depends on imports of gasoline.

Lower prices on the USGC are now needed to clear the larger gasoline surplus in that market. Lower prices make it economic to export gasoline to more distant markets, thus redefining the incremental market for USGC gasoline. Prior to 2011, USGC gasoline rarely moved to markets beyond the Americas (Figure 7). However, as the gasoline surplus in the USGC has increased, relatively lower USGC prices have been needed to make it economic to move gasoline to more distant markets. In the winter months, when U.S. gasoline demand is seasonally lowest and the surplus in the USGC peaks, USGC gasoline prices are at their lowest compared with other market hubs.

It is useful to think of the various market hubs as *"faucets"* and *"sinks."* The faucet hubs are long on product, meaning that the region produces more gasoline than can be locally consumed. The sink hubs are short product, meaning that the region consumes more gasoline than it produces. Faucet markets typically supply product to the closest sink market, minimizing transportation costs and maximizing revenue, and prices equilibrate to encourage the flow. Once demand in the closest market is satisfied, prices equilibrate to encourage supply to the next-closest market, which becomes the new marginal market.

Figure 7. U.S. Gulf Coast monthly gasoline exports by destination

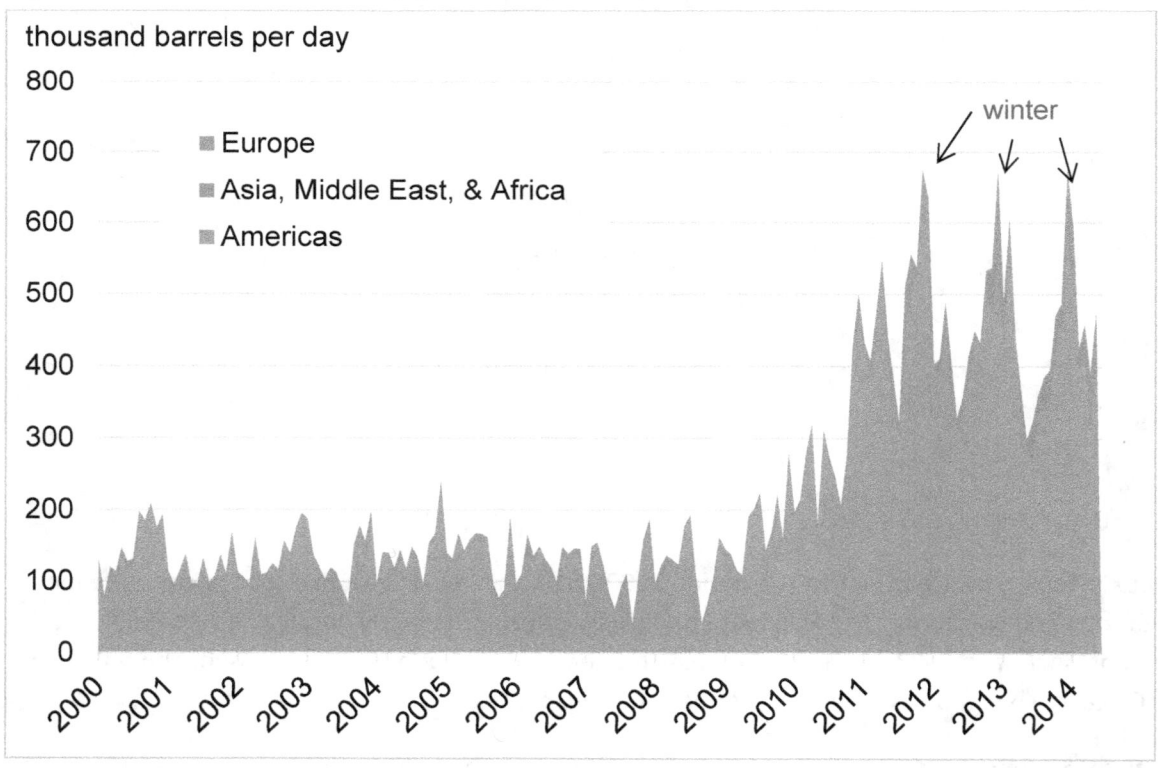

Source: U.S. Energy Information Administration, *Petroleum Supply Monthly*.

Most USGC exports of gasoline continue to supply the Americas, primarily Mexico, as it is the closest export market to the USGC. More recently, USGC exports have started to reach markets outside the Americas. The still small but growing share of exports to these markets indicates that USGC refineries have likely captured as much of the Americas gasoline market as is currently possible. As Figure 7 illustrates, demand for USGC gasoline in the Americas has been declining slowly since 2011.

With limited opportunity to increase exports to the Americas, USGC gasoline exports are moving to Africa, a market historically supplied by European refineries. In the past year, exports of gasoline from the USGC to Africa, which were historically unusual, have averaged at least 20,000 bbl/d (Figure 8). This consistent level of exports suggests that African gasoline demand is now part of the base market supplied by USGC refiners. However, the African gasoline market is relatively small, and its proximity to major refining centers in Europe and the Middle East, for which Africa is likely the marginal market, limits the potential to increase supply of U.S.-produced gasoline.

Figure 8. U.S. Gulf Coast monthly gasoline exports to Africa

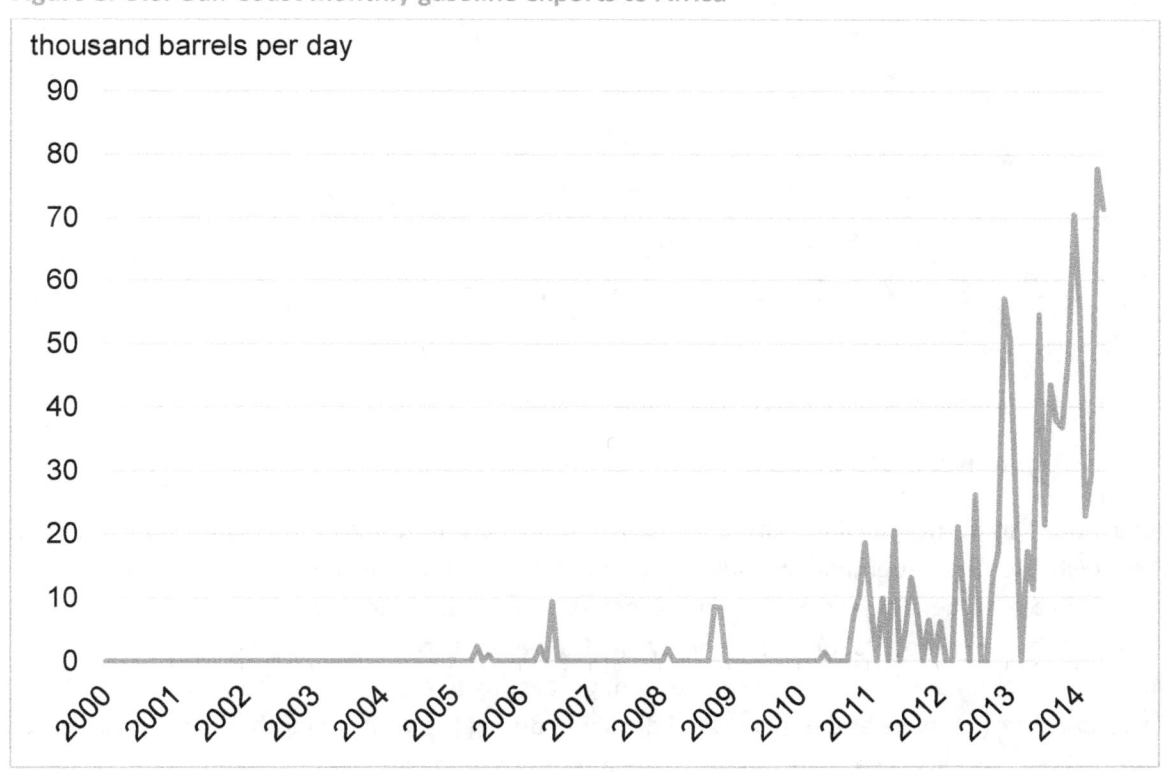

Source: U.S. Energy Information Administration, *Petroleum Supply Monthly*.

As noted earlier, USGC gasoline prices are at their lowest compared with other trading hubs during the winter months, between November and February. This deeper discount of USGC gasoline to prices in the rest of the world is needed to support sales to regions beyond the Americas and Africa. During the winter months of the past three years, the USGC has exported increasing volumes of gasoline to Asia (Figure 9), including Japan, South Korea, China, and Singapore. Exports to Asia are not economic during the U.S. summer when U.S. demand is seasonally higher and the price of gasoline in the USGC is not so steeply discounted versus prices in the rest of the world. Thus, evidence suggests that Asia is now the marginal market for USGC gasoline supplies during the winter months of November–February, while Africa is the marginal market during the balance of the year.

Figure 9. U.S. Gulf Coast monthly gasoline exports to Asia and the Middle East

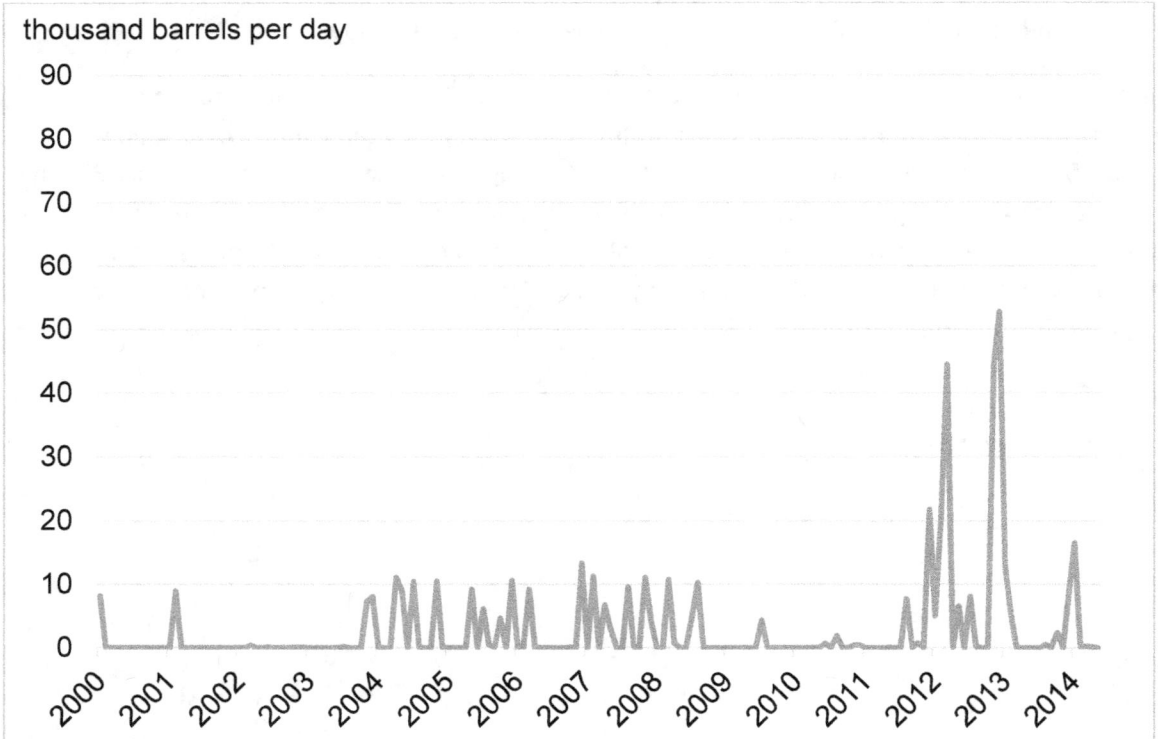

Source: U.S. Energy Information Administration, *Petroleum Supply Monthly*.

Gasoline-distillate market interactions

The foregoing analysis of the gasoline market focuses on gasoline supply and demand and does not explore how distillate supply-demand, including both diesel fuel and heating oil, affects gasoline market dynamics. Strong diesel fuel demand growth in recent years has caused diesel to price at a premium to other refined petroleum products for most of the year. The behavior of the 3-2-1 crack spread, which approximates the margin a refinery would realize from processing (cracking) three barrels of crude oil to produce two barrels of gasoline and one barrel of distillate, during the winter months when gasoline demand around the world is lowest, suggests that refineries are running the last barrel of crude oil to capture distillate margins (Figures 10 and 11). During the late autumn and early winter, gasoline margins in recent years have been very small or even negative, while distillate margins, buoyed by winter distillate demand for space heating fuel, have been strong. Without distillate demand and the contribution of distillate to refining margins, refineries might opt to reduce crude oil inputs during this time of the year, a move which would reduce the supply of gasoline in the global market and change absolute and relative gasoline prices around the world.

Figure 10. Weekly average 3-2-1 crack spreads versus Brent

Graph removed due to copyright restrictions

Source: Bloomberg LP.

Source: Distillate price used to calculate crack spread is heating oil.

Figure 11. U.S. Gulf Coast weekly average distillate and gasoline crack spreads versus Brent

Graph removed due to copyright restrictions

Source: Bloomberg LP.

Source: Distillate price used to calculate crack spread is heating oil.

Appendix: Statistical Methodology for Relationships between Gasoline and Crude Oil Price

Econometric analysis

The purpose of this analysis is to determine which benchmark light sweet crude oil (Brent or WTI) better explains (i.e., is more statistically significant in determining) gasoline spot price behavior in the various Petroleum Administration for Defense Districts (PADD) of the United States, and whether gasoline-crude oil price relationships have changed over time. To do this, EIA created models that analyze changes in gasoline spot prices as a function of changes in crude oil prices, regional inventories and crude oil price spreads. The time period chosen for the study is January 2000–June 2014. January 2011, when WTI prices first moved to a significant discount to Brent prices, offers a useful breakpoint for testing crude oil-gasoline price relationships. EIA confirmed the statistical validity of using January 2011 as a breakpoint for the data series by employing a Chow Breakpoint test. The estimated model examined the change in weekly average WTI price as a function of the change in Brent price and an error correction term (lagged WTI and lagged Brent price level). The test involved an examination of the Brent-WTI price relationship using a single model (the restricted model) for the whole time period, along with individual models (the unrestricted model) for each of the two sub-time periods (2000-10 and 2011-14), and using an F-test to compare the Sum of Squared Errors (SSE) of the restricted model with the SSE of the unrestricted model. The null hypothesis of no statistically significant change in the SSE's of the restricted and unrestricted models was rejected, indicating that January 2011 is a breakpoint in the Brent-WTI price relationship. As a result, EIA broke the data into two periods. Period 1 runs from January 2000 through December 2010, while Period 2 runs from January 2011 through June 2014.

The data analyzed consisted of Brent and WTI crude oil spot prices, regional gasoline spot prices, and regional gasoline inventories. Daily gasoline and crude oil spot prices were obtained from Bloomberg LP. The daily prices were averaged to a weekly frequency for each of the crude oils and each of the four regions with viable gasoline spot market prices: U.S. East Coast, U.S. Gulf Coast (USGC), Midwest and West Coast. These markets are represented by gasoline spot price series in: New York Harbor (NYH), USGC, Chicago (CHI), and Los Angeles (LA), respectively. To account for the effects of seasonal behavior, the regional inventories were adjusted to be deviations from the previous five-year averages.[6] The regional gasoline price series were adjusted to account for a very small number of extraordinary one-time events (e.g., Hurricane Katrina).[7]

Energy market spot price series are well known to be non-stationary in the long term, although they may demonstrate stationary behavior during short time periods.[8] To investigate the behavior of the series, EIA used autocorrelograms and augmented Dickey-Fuller (DF) tests; the results of these tests, for

---

[6] Energy Information Administration; Form EIA-800 "Weekly Refinery and Fractionator Report," Form EIA-801 "Weekly Bulk Terminal Report," Form EIA-802 "Weekly Product Pipeline Report," http://www.eia.gov/dnav/pet/pet_stoc_wstk_a_epm0_sae_mbbl_w.htm.

[7] Modified data points include Hurricane Katrina 9/2/05 (all regions); Hurricanes Gustav and Ike 9/12/08 and 9/26/08 (NYH, CHI, and USGC); Summer 2012 Chicago price spike 8/3/12 (CHI only); and 2012 California price spike 10/5/12 (LA only).

[8] A stationary series reverts to a constant, long-term mean and has a constant variance independent of time. A non-stationary series does not display these characteristics and is considered a "random walk."

the three time periods considered, are shown in Table 3. Unlike spot prices, all four of the regional gasoline inventory series demonstrate stationary behavior in both sub-time periods. The gasoline and crude oil price series are clearly non-stationary in Period 1. In Period 2, some of the test results indicate that both gasoline and crude oil prices demonstrate some stationary behavior. The time series properties of data series can be affected by the presence of major market events (e.g., the 2008 crude oil price spike) and transitory outliers principally due to weather events (especially in the gasoline price series), which make correct interpretation of the low power DF test results difficult; however, this does not appear to be the case in Period 2.

Table 3. Dickey-Fuller test and autocorrelogram results

	DF test[1]			Autocorrelogram		
	Period			Period		
	Full	1	2	Full	1	2
Inventory Deviation from 5-year avg	reject Ho	accept H1	reject Ho	stationary	stationary	stationary
Crude Oil Prices	weak accept Ho	accept Ho	reject Ho	random walk	random walk	stationary
Gasoline Prices	reject Ho	weak[2] accept Ho	reject Ho	random walk	random walk	stationary

[1]Note: "accept" means "not reject."

[2]Note: New York Harbor is "reject" in Period 1.

Because market spot price series are known to be non-stationary in the long term, EIA assumed non-stationary price series for this study. As the various combinations of crude oil and gasoline price series were found to be cointegrated by the Johansen method, EIA used error correction models (ECM) as the basis for this analytical work. Additionally, all the error correction terms in the estimated equations are significantly different from zero and are of the correct (negative) sign.

The Error Correction Term was created from the residuals (ε_t) of the following equation:

Equation 1: $y_t = \beta x_t + \text{seasonal dummy variables} + \varepsilon_t,$

where

- y_t is gasoline spot price (NYH, CHI, USGC, or LA) at time t;
- x_t is crude oil spot price (WTI or Brent) at time t.

The weekly seasonal dummy variables were defined as all weeks in a particular month. Gasoline prices demonstrate regular seasonal fluctuations; the significance test for the seasonal dummy variables shows them to be jointly different from zero.

The basic model used to investigate the regional gasoline spot price behavior was as follows:

Equation 2: $\Delta y_t = C + \Delta x' \beta + \Delta w' \tau + \gamma * \text{BWspread}_t + \lambda * \text{ECT}_{t-1} + \varepsilon_t + \text{AR(1) correction}$

U.S. Energy Information Administration | What Drives U.S. Gasoline Prices?

22

where

- $\Delta\mathbf{x}$ is a vector of current (and lagged) change in crude oil price (WTI or Brent);
- $\Delta\mathbf{w}$ is a vector of current and/or lagged change deviations from normal regional inventory;
- BWspread is the change in the Brent-WTI price differential;
- Bolded items indicate vectors.

Since the Breusch-Pagan-Godfrey test and White's test indicated the presence of residual heteroskedasticity in all of the equations, the Newey-West HAC estimator was used to calculate the covariance matrix. The expected sign of the estimated coefficient on inventory variables is negative, the expected sign on the estimated coefficient on change in crude oil price is positive with the sum equal to approximately 0.0238. The sign of the estimated coefficient on the error correction term is negative. Because gasoline prices demonstrate regular seasonal fluctuations, the significance test for the seasonal dummy variables confirmed them to be jointly different from zero.

For each of the four gasoline (mogas) spot prices considered, EIA created two different sets of equations:

1. Equation Set 1
   a. $\Delta(\text{mogas})_t = \beta_1\Delta(\text{Brent})_t + \beta_2\Delta(\text{regional inv})_t + \text{other terms}$
   b. $\Delta(\text{mogas})_t = \beta_1\Delta(\text{WTI})_t + \beta_2\Delta(\text{regional inv})_t + \text{other terms}$
2. Equation Set 2
   a. $\Delta(\text{mogas})_t = \beta_1\Delta(\text{Brent})_t + \beta_2\Delta(\text{regional inv})_t + \beta_3\Delta(\text{Brent-WTI})_t + \text{other terms}$
   b. $\Delta(\text{mogas})_t = \beta_1\Delta(\text{WTI})_t + \beta_2\Delta(\text{regional inv})_t + \beta_3\Delta(\text{Brent-WTI})_t + \text{other terms}$

where

- $\Delta(\text{Brent})$ and $\Delta(\text{WTI})$ = weekly change in Brent and WTI spot price, including lags in some cases
- $\Delta(\text{regional inv})$ = weekly change in the deviation of in-region gasoline inventories from the previous 5-year average, including lags in some cases
- $\Delta(\text{Brent-WTI})$ = weekly change in crude oil spot price differential
- Other terms include the error correction term and an AR (1) variable

These four equations were estimated for two periods:

- Period 1: January 2000–December 2010: period of narrow Brent – WTI price differentials
- Period 2: January 2011–June 2014: period of wide and variable Brent – WTI price differentials

Equation Set 1 shows changes in each of the regional gasoline spot prices as a function of the change in the respective benchmark crude oil. Comparing the results of Equations 1a and 1b will indicate whether Brent or WTI price change had more explanatory power in determining U.S. gasoline spot prices. Additionally, comparing the results of Equations 1a and 1b in Periods 1 and 2 will show whether each crude oil's explanatory power went up or down after WTI began selling at a significant discount to Brent in January 2011.

Equation Set 2 introduces the change in the Brent-WTI spread to Equation Set 1. Adding this variable allows evaluation of whether adding Brent prices to an equation that has WTI prices as an independent variable, or vice-versa, adds statistically significant explanatory power to the equation. The reasoning is as follows: if Brent is the crude oil price that explains gasoline price changes, then introducing WTI (in the form of WTI-Brent spread to reduce multicollinearity) into the gasoline/Brent estimation should add no explanatory power (i.e., result in an insignificant coefficient). However, under the same hypothesis, introducing Brent into the gasoline/WTI equation should add explanatory power (i.e., result in a statistically significant coefficient). As shown in the following section, this hypothesis is confirmed.

Results of the regression analysis

Tables 4 and 5 summarize (i.e., with the "other terms" not shown) results of the regression analysis. Tables 6 and 7 show the detailed estimation results.

Table 4. Summary regression results for Equation Set 1

Equation 1a: $\Delta(mogas) = \beta_1\Delta(Brent) + \beta_2\Delta(regional\ inv)$

Period 1: 2000-10	$\Delta(Brent)$		$\Delta(inv)^{1,2}$		Adj
	β	lags	β	lags	R-sq
New York Harbor	0.023	0	-12.0	1	0.63
U.S. Gulf Coast	0.024	0	-15.6	2	0.60
Chicago	0.023	0	-15.9	2	0.43
Los Angeles	0.024	0	-36.9	2	0.44

Equation 1a: $\Delta(mogas) = \beta_1\Delta(Brent) + \beta_2\Delta(regional\ inv)$

Period 2: 2011-14	$\Delta(Brent)$		$\Delta(inv)^{1,2}$		Adj
	β	lags	β	lags	R-sq
New York Harbor	0.023	0	-27.2	2	0.59
U.S. Gulf Coast	0.024	0	-13.0	1	0.54
Chicago	0.021	0	-20.6	1	0.37
Los Angeles	0.028	0	-41.7	2	0.44

Equation 1b: $\Delta(mogas) = \beta_1\Delta(WTI) + \beta_2\Delta(regional\ inv)$

Period 1: 2000-10	$\Delta(WTI)^{1}$		$\Delta(inv)^{1,2}$		Adj
	β	lags	β	lags	R-sq
New York Harbor	0.021	0	-11.7	1	0.58
U.S. Gulf Coast	0.021	0	-14.1	2	0.55
Chicago	0.024	1	-16.3	2	0.39
Los Angeles	0.022	0	-38.2	2	0.41

Equation 1b: $\Delta(\text{mogas}) = \beta_1 \Delta(\text{WTI}) + \beta_2 \Delta(\text{regional inv})$

Period 2: 2011-14	$\Delta(\text{WTI})^{[1]}$		$\Delta(\text{inv})^{[1,2]}$		Adj
	β	lags	β	lags	R-sq
New York Harbor	0.019	0	-20.7	1	0.42
U.S. Gulf Coast	0.020	0	-16.8	1	0.41
Chicago	0.015	0	-25.6	1	0.30
Los Angeles	0.027	1	-49.1	2	0.36

[1]Note: Where lags have been included in the equation, the reported coefficients are the sums of the lagged and present period coefficients.
[2]Note: All inventory coefficients are x10[6].

Comparing the results of Equations 1a and 1b (shown in Table 4) for both sub-time periods indicates that changes in Brent prices are more important than changes in WTI prices for all regions in explaining changes in gasoline price, as evidenced by higher R-squared values for Equation 1a for each respective gasoline spot price. Additionally, from Period 1 to Period 2 the R-squared values in Equation 1a decreased only slightly, between 0.00 and 0.06, showing the explanatory power of changes in Brent price stayed relatively unchanged. However, for WTI the R-squared values decreased between 0.05 and 0.16 from Period 1 to Period 2, showing the explanatory power of changes in WTI price went down. The lower R-squared values for both crudes in Period 2 are likely the result of changes in the U.S. gasoline market in Period 2 that reflect increasing refinery runs and declining domestic demand, which have changed historical levels and variation of U.S. gasoline-crude differentials. However, the changing nature of the U.S. gasoline market is a topic for further study.

The coefficient for change in crude oil price is expected to be approximately 0.0238 (i.e., a $1 per barrel change in the price of crude oil leads to 2.38 cents per gallon change in the price of gasoline, or 1/42). This coefficient represents full price pass-through from crude oil prices to gasoline prices. Coefficients for Brent in Period 1 are consistent with those expectations. Those coefficients change somewhat in Period 2 for Chicago and Los Angeles, likely because of differences in the nature of U.S. gasoline markets. This is responsible for the lower R-squared values described above for those hubs. For WTI, the coefficients are largely in line with expectations for Period 1, but to a lesser extent than Brent. However, in Period 2 for WTI, the coefficients deviate from the expected 0.0238 level. In both periods, the *p*-values indicate that the coefficients of both changes in Brent and WTI prices are significant at the 99% confidence level. While equations with Brent as the independent variable have higher R-squared values than those with WTI, week-to-week changes in WTI price are still very highly correlated with the week-to-week changes in Brent price, and thus with gasoline prices, even in Period 2. Additionally, the current period and lagged inventory variables are generally significant at least at the 90% confidence level across the board. (See Table 6 and 7 for details.)

For both periods and sets of equations, the R-squared values (reported in Tables 4 and 5) for New York Harbor and the USGC are higher than for Chicago and Los Angeles. This is because the Chicago and Los Angeles markets have more volatile gasoline-crude oil margins, which reflect those markets' relative isolation. Unlike New York Harbor and the USGC, they cannot directly pull supply from the actively traded Atlantic Basin, causing differentials in these markets to widen further in times of tight supply to

U.S. Energy Information Administration | What Drives U.S. Gasoline Prices?

25

encourage resupply from other more distant markets. As a result, more of the variation in gasoline price in these markets is related to price changes in the gasoline market itself, rather than changes in the price of crude oil. The inventory variable is included to capture changes in gasoline market conditions, but it is imperfect in that function. This is particularly true in markets such as Los Angeles and Chicago. For example, New York Harbor gasoline inventories comprise a significant amount of total PADD 1B (Central Atlantic) gasoline inventories, likely better reflecting supply-demand conditions in that market. However, changes in total PADD 5 (West Coast) gasoline inventory levels could vary significantly from changes in inventories in Los Angeles, as PADD 5 has several other large markets, including San Francisco, Seattle, and Portland. Thus, PADD 5 inventories might not accurately reflect gasoline market conditions in Los Angeles.

Table 5 shows regression results for Equations 2a and 2b, which include the Brent-WTI price differential as an independent variable. As discussed above, the results support the hypothesis that changes in the Brent price, rather than in the WTI price, explain changes in gasoline prices.

Table 5. Summary regression results for Equation Set 2

Equation 2a: $\Delta(\text{mogas}) = \beta_1\Delta(\text{Brent}) + \beta_2\Delta(\text{regional inv}) + \beta_3\Delta(\text{Brent-WTI})$

Period 1: 2000-10	Δ(Brent)		Δ(inv)[1,2]		Δ(Brent-WTI)		Adj
	β	lags	β	lags	β	p-value	R-sq
New York Harbor	0.023	0	-11.8	1	-0.004	0.133	0.63
U.S. Gulf Coast	0.024	0	-15.2	2	-0.004	0.236	0.60
Chicago	0.023	0	-15.9	2	0.002	0.640	0.43
Los Angeles	0.024	0	-36.9	2	-0.004	0.410	0.44

Equation 2a: $\Delta(\text{mogas}) = \beta_1\Delta(\text{Brent}) + \beta_2\Delta(\text{regional inv}) + \beta_3\Delta(\text{Brent-WTI})$

Period 2: 2011-14	Δ(Brent)		Δ(inv)[1,2]		Δ(Brent-WTI)		Adj
	β	lags	β	lags	β	p-value	R-sq
New York Harbor	0.024	0	-27.2	2	0.000	0.955	0.59
U.S. Gulf Coast	0.025	0	-13.6	1	-0.005	0.124	0.55
Chicago	0.021	0	-20.6	1	-0.001	0.883	0.37
Los Angeles	0.030	0	-44.7	2	-0.008	0.096	0.45

Equation 2b: Δ(mogas) = $\beta_1\Delta$(WTI) + $\beta_2\Delta$(regional inv) + $\beta_3\Delta$(Brent-WTI)

Period 1: 2000-10	Δ(WTI)		Δ(inv)[1,2]		Δ(Brent-WTI)		Adj
	β	lags	β	lags	β	p-value	R-sq
New York Harbor	0.023	0	-12.0	1	0.017	0.000	0.63
U.S. Gulf Coast	0.024	0	-15.1	2	0.018	0.000	0.60
Chicago	0.023	0	-15.0	2	0.022	0.000	0.43
Los Angeles	0.024	0	-17.5	2	0.019	0.000	0.44

Equation 2b: Δ(mogas) = $\beta_1\Delta$(WTI) + $\beta_2\Delta$(regional inv) + $\beta_3\Delta$(Brent-WTI)

Period 2: 2011-14	Δ(WTI)		Δ(inv)[1,2]		Δ(Brent-WTI)		Adj
	β	lags	β	Lags	β	p-value	R-sq
New York Harbor	0.023	0	-14.6	1	0.020	0.000	0.54
U.S. Gulf Coast	0.023	0	-15.6	1	0.017	0.000	0.50
Chicago	0.018	0	-23.0	1	0.016	0.000	0.33
Los Angeles	0.028	0	-37.3	1	0.020	0.000	0.41

[1]Note: Where lags have been included in the equations, the reported coefficients are sums of the lagged and present period coefficients.

[2]Note: All inventory coefficients are x10^6.

For Equation 2a, the coefficients on the Brent and inventory variables are largely unchanged, for the different markets and time periods, from Equation 1a. Importantly, the addition of the change in the price differential between Brent and WTI does not add explanatory power to the Brent equations. The coefficients of the Brent-WTI spread in Equation 2a are insignificant with the exception of Los Angeles in Period 2, which is barely significant at the 90% level. In this case, the coefficient is likely picking up other trends in the data, as the Los Angeles gasoline market is not meaningfully connected to the WTI market. Additionally, the R-squared values for Equation 2a are generally unchanged from Equation 1a. This indicates that including the spread between Brent and WTI prices adds no explanatory power to the change in gasoline price when Brent is already an independent variable. However, the addition of the price spread between Brent and WTI prices does add explanatory power to the WTI equations (Equation 2b in Table 5). The coefficients of the Brent-WTI spread in Equation 2b are all significant at the 99% confidence level. Furthermore, the R-squared values for Equation 2b all exceed those for Equation 1b. That Brent adds explanatory power to the WTI equations, but not vice-versa, is a particularly important result. This evidence supports the conclusion that the price of Brent, rather than the price of WTI, is the more important crude oil in determining U.S. gasoline prices.

Tables 6 and 7 present a detailed version of the regression results.

Table 6. Detailed regression results for Equation Set 1

New York Harbor	Period 1 (Jan 2000 - Dec 2010)				Period 2 (Jan 2011 - Jun 2014)			
dependent var	Δ mg_ny		Δ mg_ny		Δ mg_ny		Δ mg_ny	
equation	1a		1b		1a		1b	
constant	0.000		0.001		0.000		0.002	
Δ brent	0.023	***			0.023	***		
Δ wti			0.021	***			0.019	***
Δ dsa_stock	-4.3E-06	**	-4.6E-06	**	-6.5E-06		-1.0E-05	**
Δ dsa_stock(-1)	-7.7E-06	***	-7.1E-06	***	-1.1E-05	***	-1.1E-05	**
Δ dsa_stock(-2)					-1.0E-05	**		
ECT(-1)	-0.152	***	-0.126	***	-0.395	***	-0.144	***
AR(1)	0.171	**	0.136	**	0.368	**	0.184	*
no. obs.	571		571		178		178	
adj. R^2	0.627		0.576		0.593		0.417	
S.E. regression	0.046		0.049		0.058		0.069	

Note: Significance level indicators are * at the 10%, ** at the 5%, and *** at the 1% level.

Gulf Coast	Period 1 (Jan 2000 - Dec 2010)				Period 2 (Jan 2011 - Jun 2014)			
dependent var	Δ mg_gc		Δ mg_gc		Δ mg_gc		Δ mg_gc	
equation	1a		1b		1a		1b	
constant	0.001		0.001		-0.001		-0.000	
Δ brent	0.024	***			0.024	***		
Δ wti			0.021	***			0.020	***
Δ dsa_stock	-6.5E-06	***	-5.3E-06	**	-6.4E-06	*	-9.0E-06	**
Δ dsa_stock(-1)	-4.2E-06	***	-3.4E-06	**	-6.6E-06	**	-7.8E-06	**
Δ dsa_stock(-2)	-4.9E-06	***	-5.34E-06	***				
ECT(-1)	-0.148	***	-0.137	***	-0.386	***	-0.182	***
AR(1)	0.161	**	0.141	**	0.256	**	0.223	*
no. obs.	570		570		178		178	
adj. R^2	0.602		0.553		0.543		0.414	
S.E. regression	0.050		0.053		0.063		0.072	

Note: Significance level indicators are * at the 10%, ** at the 5%, and *** at the 1% level.

Chicago	Period 1 (Jan 2000 - Dec 2010)		Period 2 (Jan 2011 - Jun 2014)	
dependent var	Δ mg_chi	Δ mg_chi	Δ mg_chi	Δ mg_chi
equation	1a	1b	1a	1b
constant	0.000	0.000	0.001	0.003
Δ brent	0.023 ***		0.021 ***	
Δ wti		0.0193 ***		0.015 ***
Δ wti(-1)		0.0044 ***		
Δ dsa_stock	-4.4E-06 *	-4.2E-06 *		
Δ dsa_stock(-1)	-7.3E-06 ***	-7.0E-06 **	-2.1E-05 ***	-2.6E-05 ***
Δ dsa_stock(-2)	-4.2E-06 *	-5.2E-06 **		
ECT(-1)	-0.185 ***	-0.1615 ***	-0.572 ***	-0.460 ***
AR(1)	0.143 **	0.1041 *	0.359 ***	0.340 **
no. obs.	570	570	179	179
adj. R^2	0.426	0.385	0.375	0.300
S.E. regression	0.072	0.074	0.107	0.113

Note: Significance level indicators are * at the 10%, ** at the 5%, and *** at the 1% level.

Los Angeles	Period 1 (Jan 2000 - Dec 2010)		Period 2 (Jan 2011 - Jun 2014)	
dependent var	Δ mg_la	Δ mg_la	Δ mg_la	Δ mg_la
equation	1a	1b	1a	1b
constant	0.000	0.000	0.000	0.001
Δ brent	0.024 ***		0.028 ***	
Δ wti		0.022 ***		0.023 ***
Δ wti(-1)				0.004
Δ dsa_stock	-9.8E-06 **	-9.7E-06 **	-1.3E-05	-1.2E-05
Δ dsa_stock(-1)	-1.6E-05 ***	-1.8E-05 ***	-1.6E-05	-2.3E-05 **
Δ dsa_stock(-2)	-1.1E-05 ***	-1.1E-05 ***	-1.3E-05	-1.4E-05
ECT(-1)	-0.176 ***	-0.174 ***	-0.361 ***	-0.254 ***
AR(1)	0.195 ***	0.203 ***	0.146	0.158
no. obs.	565	565	178	178
adj. R^2	0.441	0.409	0.445	0.361
S.E. regression	0.075	0.077	0.095	0.102

Note: Significance level indicators are * at the 10%, ** at the 5%, and *** at the 1% level.

Table 7. Detailed regression results for Equation Set 2

New York Harbor	Period 1 (Jan 2000 - Dec 2010)				Period 2 (Jan 2011 - Jun 2014)			
dependent var	Δ mg_ny		Δ mg_ny		Δ mg_ny		Δ mg_ny	
equation	2a		2b		2a		2b	
constant	0.000		0.000		0.002		0.001	***
Δ brent	0.023	***			0.024	***		
Δ wti			0.023	***			0.023	***
Δ dsa_stock	-4.2E-06	**	-4.2E-06	**	0.000		-7.4E-06	*
Δ dsa_stock(-1)	-7.6E-06	***	-7.3E-06	***	-1.1E-05	***	-7.3E-06	*
Δ dsa_stock(-2)					-1.0E-05	*		
Δ brent-wti	-0.004		0.017	***	-0.000		0.020	***
ECT(-1)	-0.147	***	-0.123	***	-0.393	***	-0.126	**
AR(1)	0.163	**	0.154	**	0.366	**	0.190	*
no. obs.	571		571		178		178	
adj. R^2	0.630		0.625		0.590		0.542	
S.E. regression	0.046		0.046		0.058		0.061	

Note: Significance level indicators are * at the 10%, ** at the 5%, and *** at the 1% level.

Gulf Coast	Period 1 (Jan 2000 - Dec 2010)				Period 2 (Jan 2011 - Jun 2014)			
dependent var	Δ mg_gc		Δ mg_gc		Δ mg_gc		Δ mg_gc	
equation	2a		2b		2a		2b	
constant	0.001		0.001		-0.001		-0.001	
Δ brent	0.024	***			0.025	***		
Δ wti			0.024	***			0.023	***
Δ dsa_stock	-6.3E-06	***	-6.4E-06	***	-6.8E-06	*	-8.3E-06	**
Δ dsa_stock(-1)	-4.0E-06	***	-3.9E-06	***	-6.9E-06	**	-7.3E-06	**
Δ dsa_stock(-2)	-4.9E-06	***	-4.8E-06	***				
Δ brent-wti	-0.004		0.018	***	-0.005		0.017	***
ECT(-1)	-0.144	***	-0.132	***	-0.382	***	-0.140	**
AR(1)	0.154	**	0.149	**	0.260	**	0.149	
no. obs.	570		570		178		178	
adj. R^2	0.604		0.602		0.547		0.333	
S.E. regression	0.050		0.050		0.063		0.110	

Note: Significance level indicators are * at the 10%, ** at the 5%, and *** at the 1% level.

Chicago	Period 1 (Jan 2000 - Dec 2010)				Period 2 (Jan 2011 - Jun 2014)			
dependent var	Δ mg_chi		Δ mg_chi		Δ mg_chi		Δ mg_chi	
equation	2a		2b		2a		2b	
constant	0.000		0.000		0.001		0.003	
Δ brent	0.023	***			0.021	***		
Δ wti			0.023	***			0.018	***
Δ wti(-1)			0.003	**				
Δ dsa_stock	-4.5E-06	*	-4.4E-06	*				
Δ dsa_stock(-1)	-7.3E-06	***	-7.0E-06	**	-2.1E-05	***	-2.3E-05	***
Δ dsa_stock(-2)	-4.1E-06	*	0.000					
Δ brent-wti	0.002		0.022	***	-0.001		0.016	***
ECT(-1)	-0.189	***	-0.172	***	-0.570	***	-0.515	***
AR(1)	0.152	**	0.152	**	0.357	***	0.417	***
no. obs.	570		570		179		179	
adj. R^2	0.426		0.432		0.371		0.333	
S.E. regression	0.072		0.071		0.107		0.110	

Note: Significance level indicators are * at the 10%, ** at the 5%, and *** at the 1% level.

Los Angeles	Period 1 (Jan 2000 - Dec 2010)				Period 2 (Jan 2011 - Jun 2014)			
dependent var	Δ mg_la		Δ mg_la		Δ mg_la		Δ mg_la	
equation	2a		2b		2a		2b	
constant	0.000		0.000		0.000		0.000	
Δ brent	0.024	***			0.030	***		
Δ wti			0.024	***			0.028	***
Δ wti(-1)								
Δ dsa_stock	-9.8E-06	**	-1.0E-05	***	0.000		-1.8E-05	*
Δ dsa_stock(-1)	-1.7E-05	***	-1.7E-05	***	-1.8E-05	*	-1.9E-05	*
Δ dsa_stock(-2)	-1.1E-05	***	-1.1E-05	***	0.000			
Δ brent-wti	-0.004		0.019	***	-0.008	*	0.020	***
ECT(-1)	-0.176	***	-0.164	***	-0.290	***	-0.170	***
AR(1)	0.197	***	0.191	***				
no. obs.	565		565		179		179	
adj. R^2	0.442		0.441		0.447		0.413	
S.E. regression	0.075		0.075		0.095		0.098	

Note: Significance level indicators are * at the 10%, ** at the 5%, and *** at the 1% level.

Dynamic linear modeling

Further evidence of the importance of Brent in determining U.S. gasoline prices is found by investigating parameter behavior over time using Dynamic Linear Modeling (DLM). Previous analysis found that market conditions changed due to major exogenous changes to the crude oil and/or gasoline distribution structure; this occurred on or about January 2011. This exercise determines whether or not the model coefficients significantly changed during the analysis period. A simplified model was employed using only current variables analyzing spot gasoline price as a function of crude oil price, PADD level gasoline inventory (adjusted for seasonal patterns), and the Brent/WTI spread.

The models (for NYH spot gasoline price) were

Brent:

$$mga\_ny_t = \alpha + \beta_t(Brent_t) + \delta_t(P1B\_Inv_t) + \omega_t(BWspread_t) + \varepsilon_t$$

$$\beta_{t+1} = \beta_t + v_t$$

$$\omega_{t+1} = \omega_t + \eta_t$$

WTI:

$$mga\_ny_t = \alpha + \beta_t(WTI_t) + \delta_t(P1B\_Inv_t) + \omega_t(BWspread_t) + \varepsilon_t$$

$$\beta_{t+1} = \beta_t + v_t$$

$$\omega_{t+1} = \omega_t + \eta_t$$

where

- mga_ny_t = NYH spot gasoline price at time t;
- (Brent) and (WTI) = Brent and WTI spot prices at time t;
- (P1B_Inv) = deviation of in-region gasoline inventories from 5-year average at time t;
- (BWspread) = crude oil spot price differential (Brent − WTI) at time t; and
- ε_t, v_t, and η_t are normally distributed random error series.

In this study, the behavior of inventories was not of interest and was not dynamically analyzed.

The results of the New York Harbor model estimation are shown as graphs of smoothed state estimates for the coefficient on crude oil (Figures 12 and 13) and for the coefficient on the Brent/WTI spread (Figure 14 for Brent and Figure 15 for WTI). The figures also show confidence bands of $\pm$ 2 RMSE, where RMSE is the root mean squared error.

As expected, the crude oil coefficients (SV1 state variable) for both models are very similar, and vary by a value of about 0.25 over the entire time period. However, what is noticeable is that the state estimated standard errors for the period beginning in January 2011 are much larger than for the earlier period. These results show that the relationship between crude oil price changes and gasoline price changes fluctuates over the analysis period (coefficient range is 0.19 to 0.34) and that the gasoline price change is similar for both crude oils. The latter result is not surprising, given that the correlation between the two crude oil prices is 0.98.

Figures 14 and 15 show the changing relationship (SV3 state variable) over time between gasoline prices and the WTI/Brent crude oil price spread. Both state estimates show a significant decrease during the analysis time period (from 0.015 to 0.003 for the Brent model and -0.010 to -0.020 for the WTI model). The estimated coefficient reached its largest value at the time that the crude oil market began its recovery after the dramatic collapse late in 2008. The important thing to note is that in the Brent model, the coefficient is statistically different from zero from January 2000 to the middle of 2006, and is insignificant thereafter. In contrast, the coefficient in the WTI model is statistically less than zero for the entire time period, with the coefficient becoming larger in absolute value over time. These results seem to imply that while Brent was the crude oil determining gasoline price in the recent period, both (or other) crudes impacted gasoline prices in the earlier period.

Figure 12 (appendix). Brent model, crude oil coefficient

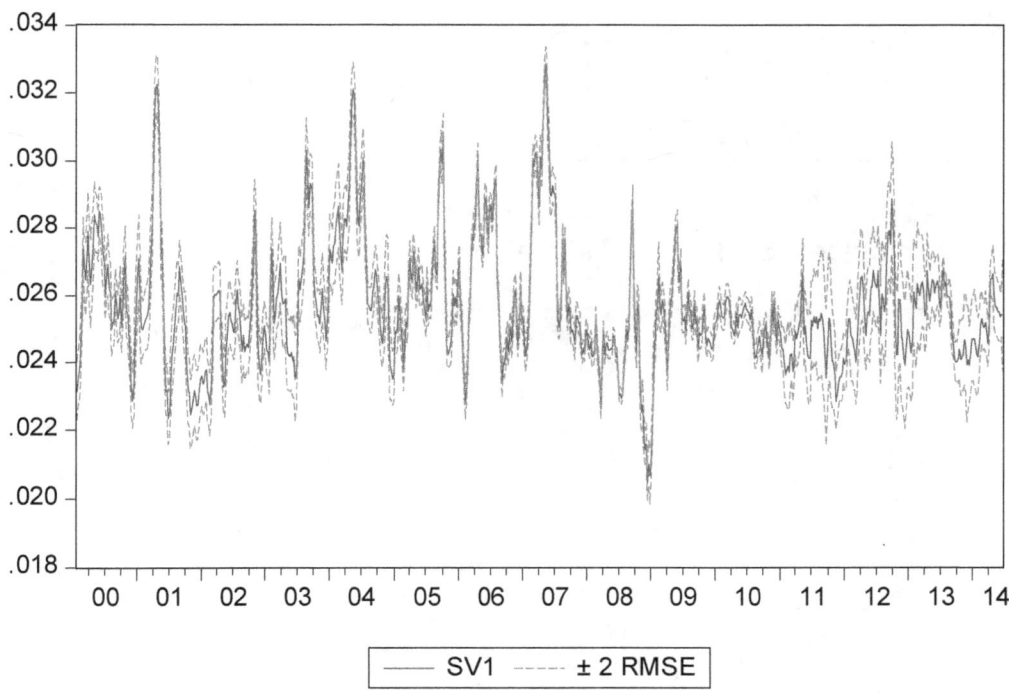

Smoothed SV1 State Estimate

Figure 13 (appendix). WTI model, crude oil coefficient

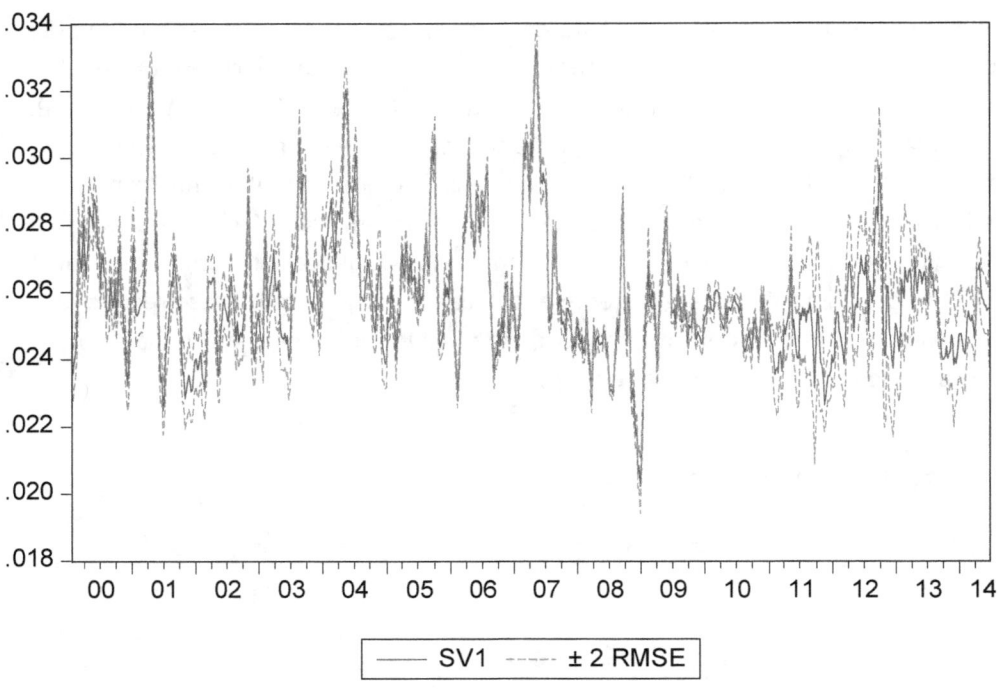

Smoothed SV1 State Estimate

Figure 14 (appendix). PADD 1B (NYH): Brent model, spread coefficient

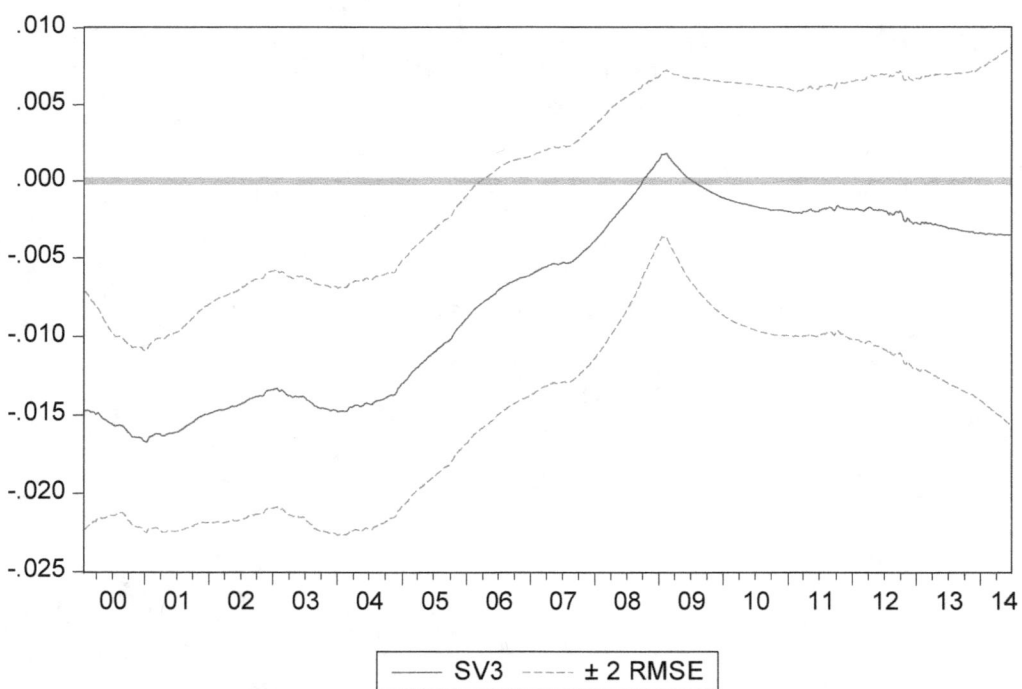

Smoothed SV3 State Estimate

Figure 15 (appendix). PADD 1B (NYH): WTI model, spread coefficient

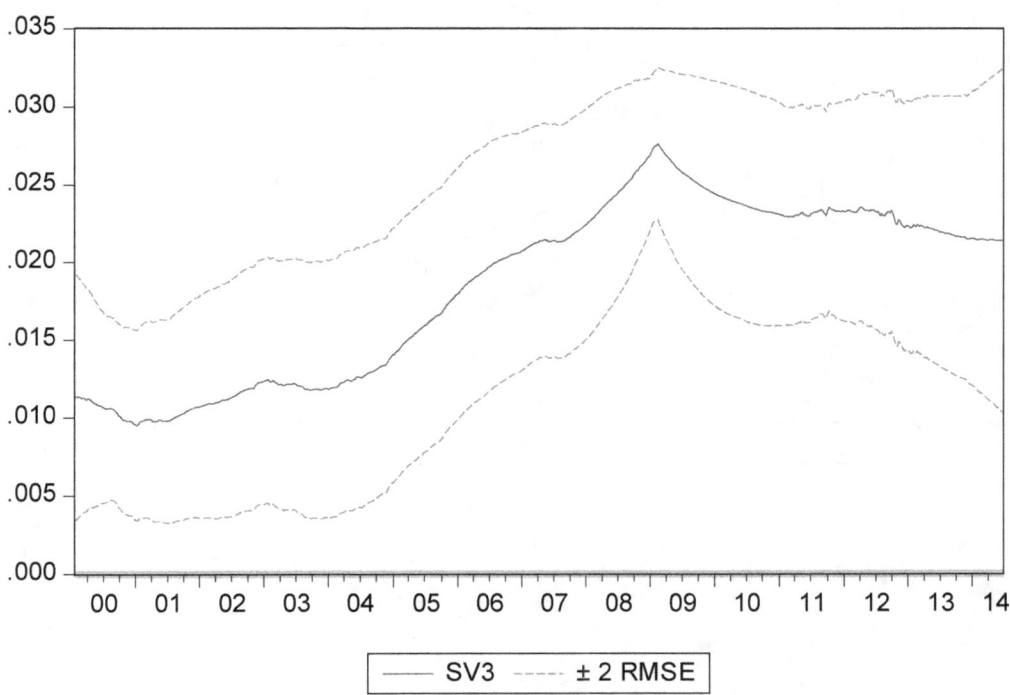

Smoothed SV3 State Estimate

The estimation results for the other regions show similar results (Figures 16-18). The shift of the crude oil coefficients (SV1 coefficient) around 2008 is similar to the coefficient shift in PADD 1B. Additionally, in PADD 2 (Midwest), the spread coefficient (SV3) is insignificant in the Brent model for most of the analysis period. PADD 3 (Gulf Coast) and PADD 5 (West Coast) differ from the other regions in that the spread coefficient (SV3) is not significantly different from zero for most of the first half of the sample period.

Figure 16 (appendix). PADD 2: Chicago spot

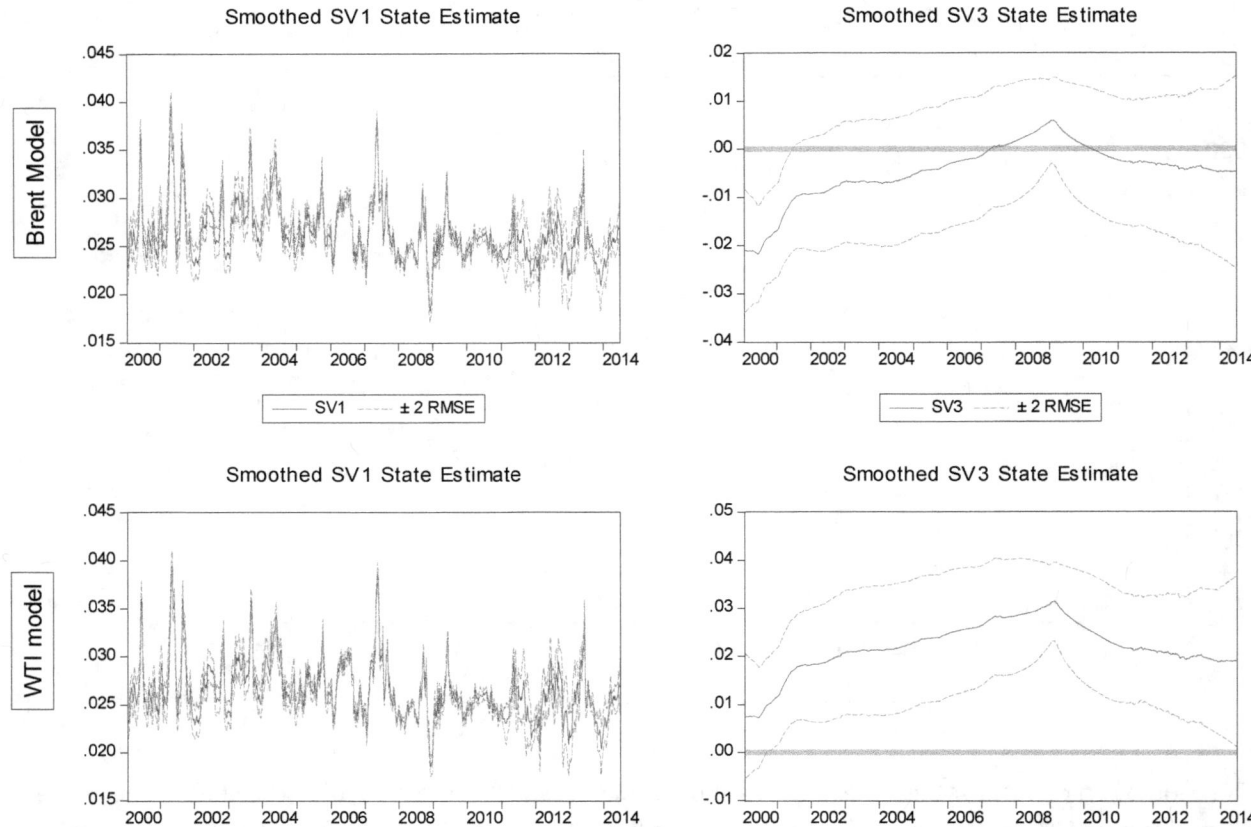

U.S. Energy Information Administration | What Drives U.S. Gasoline Prices?

36

Figure 17 (appendix). PADD 3: Gulf Coast spot

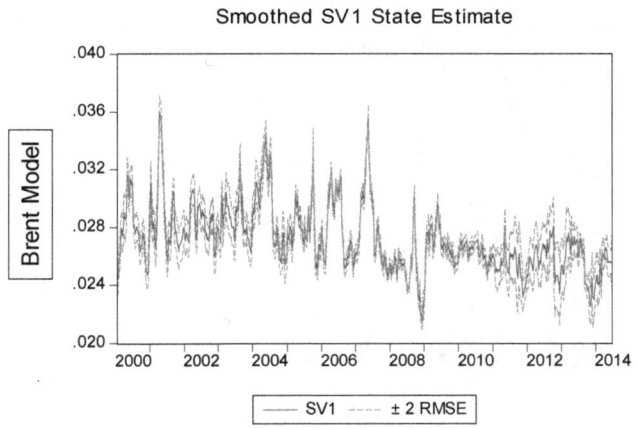
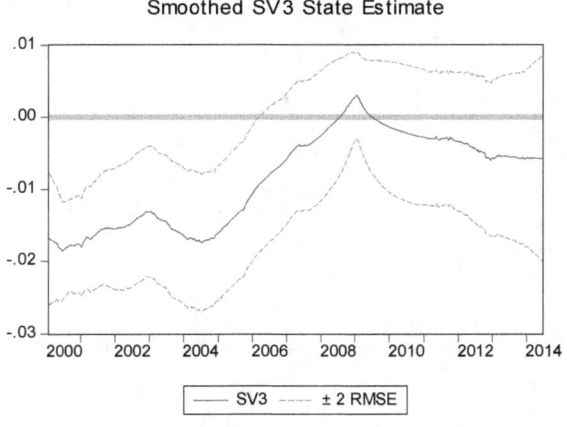
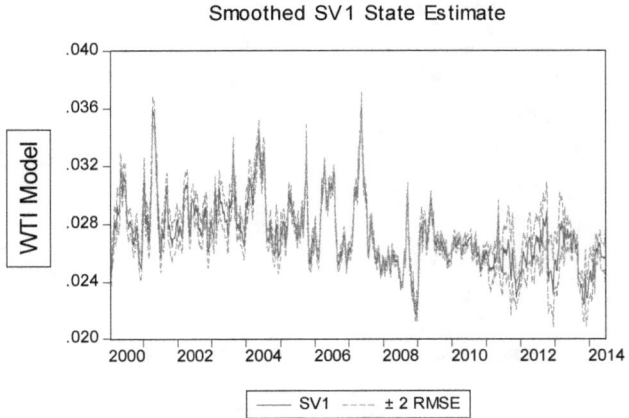
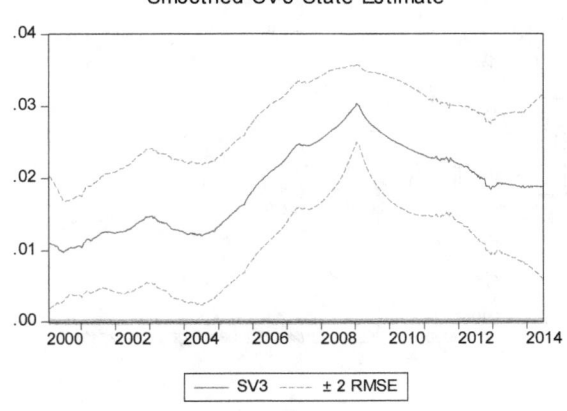

U.S. Energy Information Administration | What Drives U.S. Gasoline Prices?

37

Figure 18 (appendix). PADD 5: Los Angeles spot

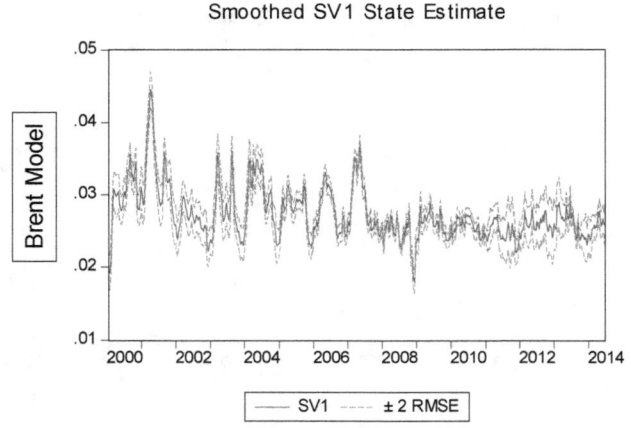

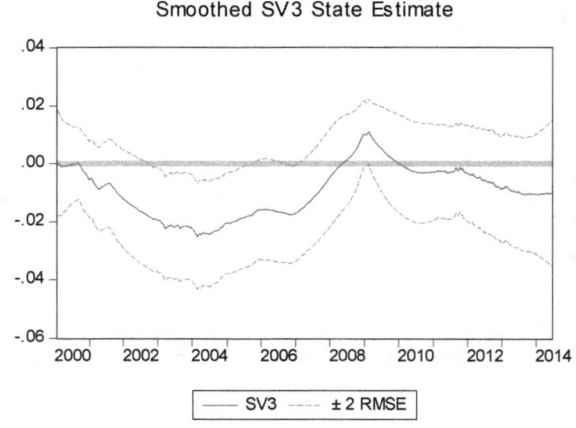

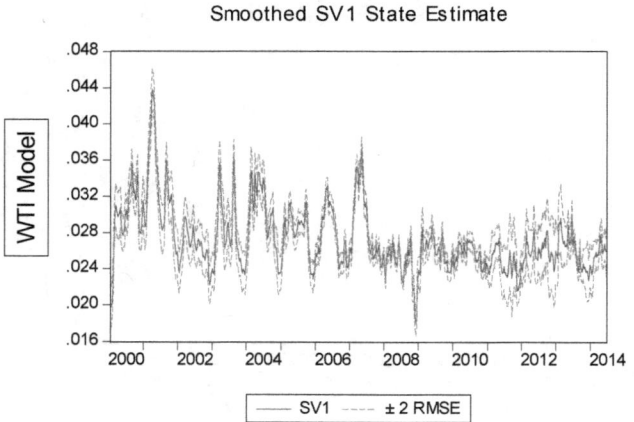

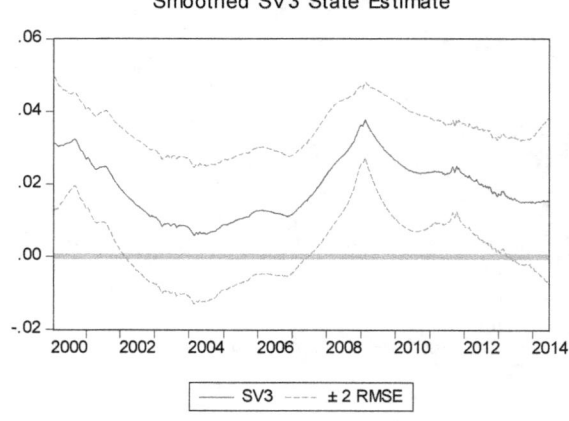

www.ingramcontent.com/pod-product-compliance
Lightning Source LLC
Chambersburg PA
CBHW081129280526
45787CB00007B/3030